AF406274

Through Fire and Faith

A Woman's True Story of Survival, Cancer, Poverty, and God's Unfailing Presence

Evelyn Abiagom

Dedication

This book is dedicated to the Lord Jesus Christ.

From a very young age, He revealed Himself to me in a way that changed my life forever. At just twelve years old, in a time of loss and uncertainty after my mother's passing, I encountered Him in a deeply personal and unforgettable way.

In a moment when I felt alone and without direction, He came to me—not just as a distant figure, but as a real and present Savior. The experience was so powerful, so personal, that it filled my heart with a joy I could not contain and a love I had never known before.

From that day on, my life was never the same.

Even now, I carry that encounter in my heart. It drew me closer to Him, shaped my faith, and became the foundation of my journey. Not everyone may experience Him in the same way I did, but I know without a doubt that He is real, that He loves us, and that He reaches out to us in ways we may not always expect.

This book is my offering to Him—my gratitude, my testimony, and my acknowledgment of His presence in every chapter of my life. All that I am, and all that I have overcome, is because of Him.

Acknowledgment

First and foremost, I give all thanks and glory to God for His mercy, His love, and His faithfulness in my life. Without Him, I would not be here today. Every step of this journey has been sustained by His grace.

I would also like to express my deepest gratitude to my husband, **Hilary Abiagom**, who stood by me during some of the most difficult moments of my life. Even when there was little or nothing materially, he remained steadfast in prayer and unwavering in his support. His presence meant more than words can express.

I am also grateful to the pastors and spiritual leaders who came into my life during my time of illness. During my chemotherapy, many of them visited, prayed, and stood in faith with me. Though I may not remember all their names, their kindness, prayers, and encouragement left a lasting impact on my heart.

To each and every one of you, I say thank you. Your presence in my journey was not by chance, but by God's divine arrangement

__Introduction__

This book is not just a story—it is a testimony.

It is written for someone, somewhere, who may be going through difficult moments in life and is searching for hope, understanding, or simply a reason to keep believing. If you are that person, I want you to know this: the same God who was there for me is there for you.

There were times in my life when everything seemed uncertain, when challenges surrounded me, and when it felt like I was alone. But through it all, God was constant—faithful as the rising sun, ever-present, and never distant. Even when I thought He was far away, He was right there beside me.

What I have come to understand is that knowing God is deeply personal. It is not just about attending church or saying long, perfect prayers. Sometimes, it is in the simplest, most honest words spoken from the heart that we truly connect with Him. God sees the heart. He knows our struggles, our fears, and our desires, and He is always ready to listen.

There were moments when I longed for Him, when I cried out, "Lord, I miss You," and in those moments, I felt His presence in ways I cannot fully explain. That relationship—real, personal, and alive—is something I wish for everyone to experience.

This book is my way of saying thank You to God for everything He has done in my life. It is by His mercy that I am here today. There were situations I went through where, by all human understanding, I should not have made it. Yet, He kept me. He provided for me. He protected me. He carried me through.

If my story can encourage even one person to call on God, to trust Him, and to believe that He is still near, then this book has fulfilled its purpose.

1

My life did not begin with a calling. It began with loss, confusion, and questions I did not know how to ask. I was not looking for God. I was a child doing what I was told—going to school, going to church, following rules that did not explain the ache I carried inside me. I did not know there was a difference between knowing *about* God and knowing Him. I did not even know such a distinction existed. But something began to unfold when I was young, quietly at first, without instruction or preparation, and it never stopped. This is not a story I learned to tell. It is a story that happened to me.

My first encounter with the Lord Jesus Christ happened in 1976. I remember the year clearly because it marked a turning point I did not understand at the time. I was still in boarding school then. It was a mixed school, boys and girls together, full of noise, laughter, restlessness. We were young, carefree in the way children can be when they do not yet know what life will ask of them.

There was a boy in my class who stood out, though not in the way people usually stand out. He was quiet. While the rest of us jumped around, talked endlessly, and found ways to misbehave, he remained still. He watched more than he spoke. There was something about him that did not fit into the rhythm of the rest of us.

At first, I did not know why I noticed him. I only knew that I did.

One day, I went up to him and asked directly, as children often do. I said, "Why are you like this? Why are you different?" He did not seem offended. He said he was a Christian.

I laughed and told him we were all Christians. We went to church. We attended Sunday school. Christianity was part of our routine. It was part of our environment. It did not feel like something you *became*. It was something you inherited.

He told me his Christianity was different. He said he knew the Lord Jesus Christ.

I did not understand what that meant. I told him I also knew Jesus. I could recite prayers. I went to church. I followed the rules. But something about his answer stayed with me. I began to watch him more closely. I could not explain it, but I sensed that whatever he had was not something I had learned.

Not long after that, I began to dream.

The first night, I saw a bright light. It was not the kind of light you see from a lamp or the sun. It was intense, pure, and overwhelming. In that light, I saw the cross. There were no words spoken. Just the image, clear and unmistakable.

The second night, the dream continued.

I saw the Lord Jesus Christ.

He came into the school compound, into a place I recognized. He was seated on a small stone in the playground. Around Him, everything went on as usual. Children were running, shouting, playing. No one seemed to notice Him. But I did.

I was standing apart, leaning against the railing of one of the buildings. When I saw Him, I knew who He was without being told. I said to myself, *That is Christ.* I wanted to go closer. I wanted to meet Him.

As I walked toward Him, I noticed what He was wearing—red and white clothing, sandals on His feet. He was handsome in a way that felt gentle, not overwhelming. When I reached Him, before I could speak, He called my name.

"Evelyn."

I had not told Him who I was. He said, "I know what you are looking for, and you will surely find it."

That was all.

He stood up and began to walk away. I followed Him, but I could not get close. He was walking at a normal pace, yet there was a flame coming from Him—light and fire together. I did not know what to call it. I only knew I could not draw nearer. I stayed behind Him, following as best I could.

He entered a building, and I could not see Him anymore.

Suddenly, I found myself in a large hall. There was a long table, and on it lay a very big book, opened wide. The edges of the pages looked worn, almost pierced, as if they had holes in them. At that time, I was not a Bible reader. No one had taught me Scripture. I did not know verses by heart.

Then a voice spoke.

"For God so loved the world, that He gave His only begotten Son, that whosoever believes in Him will not perish, but have everlasting life."

I woke up from the dream.

Later, I heard another voice, as if from a distance, calling my name again. It said, "Evelyn, you've got life."

When I woke fully, something had changed inside me. All the heaviness I carried—burdens I did not even know how to describe—were gone. I felt light, free, confused, and alive all at once. I kept saying out loud, "I've got life. I've got life."

That same year, my mother died.

I went to spend a weekend at a friend's house shortly after. When I came out of the room the next morning, the woman of the house looked at me and was startled. She asked what had happened to me. I did not know how to explain it. I said, "It's Jesus." That was all I could say.

Everything about me had changed. When I went to get my hair done before returning to school, the woman refused. She said something was different about me. I walked along the road telling strangers, "Jesus loves you," without thinking about how it sounded.

At home, after my mother's death, my father remarried. We were afraid of our stepmother. None of us were close to her. We were sent to boarding school, partly to keep the peace, partly because no one knew what to do with us.

I would go to an unfinished building near the house when the pain became too much. I cried there. I prayed there, though I did not know what prayer was supposed to look like. Sometimes the air around me would change. The sunlight would grow brighter, colors more vivid. I did not know then that God was speaking to me. No one had preached Christ to me. No one had explained what was happening.

He continued to come.

Once, I saw Him again in the school garden. This time I was awake. I was not dreaming. He showed me the nail prints in His hands and feet. His feet did not touch the ground. His body was beautiful. The wounds looked fresh, as if the crucifixion had just happened.

After these encounters, I began to read the Bible. I wanted to understand the One who had come to me without being invited.

I did not know then that this was only the beginning.

After those early encounters, I could not return to being the person I had been before. I was still young, still uncertain, but something in me had already shifted. I wanted to know God, not as an idea, but as the One who had already come looking for me.

I began to read the Bible slowly. I was not guided by any special teacher. I read because I felt drawn to it. The words felt alive. It was not like reading for school. It felt like being spoken to, corrected, comforted, and sometimes challenged.

People around me noticed the change. When I visited home, my stepmother said I was no longer the same. My father asked what had happened to me. I told him simply, "It is Christ." That became my only explanation. I did not have language for anything more complicated.

There were moments when God's presence felt near in ways I could not explain. Once, I saw Him in what looked like Egypt, surrounded by pyramids. He told me I could not escape His presence, that even if I tried to run, I would still find Him. He spoke calmly, without threat, without pressure. He simply stated what was.

After completing my West African School Certificate examinations, I did not obtain the grades required for immediate university admission. It was a painful setback. While many of my peers moved forward, I remained behind, preparing to retake the examinations. I worked for a year during that period, studying again and hoping for another opportunity.

At the time, I was already engaged. My fiancé — who is now my husband — had gained admission into the University of Ife in the western part of Nigeria. He was academically ahead of me and deeply involved in campus Christian activities. Eventually, he became President of the Christian Union. He was well known, respected, and constantly surrounded by fellow students.

I visited him at the university during that season. While I was there, one of his friends told me that he intended to marry another girl on campus. I did not confront him. I lacked the confidence. I had not yet secured my own admission. I already felt academically behind and insecure. I carried the pain silently.

I returned to Lagos heartbroken. From Surulere, I entered a taxi heading toward Victoria Island with one intention — to end my life. As the taxi moved, something happened that I still cannot fully explain. It was not warm. It was cold. I felt something cold pour over my head. I could not see it. I could not physically touch it. But I felt it flow.

Instantly, the heavy burden to kill myself lifted.

When the taxi reached Victoria Island, I went to the beach and sat watching the dolphins in the distance. I did not enter the water. After some time, I returned home.

Later, I heard a voice say, "It's a lie, my daughter." The weight left me. I did not argue with what I heard. I simply kept going.

At another time, while walking along Bode Thomas Street, Surulere, Lagos, a voice called my name. When I turned, no one was there. Then the voice said, "I am the God of all flesh. Is anything too difficult for Me to do?" I knelt by the roadside and cried. I had not known God could speak so directly.

Life did not become easier after that.

There were years of deep financial hardship. We could not pay rent. We could not afford school fees. Our children stopped going to school. Many times, I locked them inside the house so neighbors would not know how bad things were. We ate whatever small thing came in. There was no stability. Only survival.

One year stands out clearly—1997, around Christmas.

In our community, Christmas is a loud season. Children play outside. They throw fireworks. They wear new clothes. That year, my children could not join them because we had no money. I kept them indoors. I was ashamed. I was angry. I was desperate.

We kept hoping that something would come in before Christmas—money to buy food, clothes, anything. Nothing came.

On the evening of the 23rd or 24th, my husband came home with nothing. I lost control. I slapped him. I cried. I told him that before I married him, I had always celebrated Christmas in my father's house, and now my children had nothing. I said things out of pain. The children did not understand what I was saying. I am not sure I did either.

My husband left the house without arguing.

Later, he returned, crying.

My son told me, "Mommy, Daddy is crying." I said he deserved to cry. I said he had failed us. I spoke out of hurt and frustration.

Then he reached into his pocket and brought out a very small, tightly rolled piece of paper. When he opened it, it was one hundred US dollars.

At that time, the exchange rate was 11,760 naira.

He told me he had gone out to buy shaving supplies. As he stepped out of the car, his toe hit a stone on the ground and he almost fell. Something told him to pick up what was in front of his foot and put it in his pocket without opening it. He obeyed. When he opened it at home, it was the money.

He told me God said he should give it to me.

I went out immediately. I bought secondhand clothes for the children. I bought rice, chicken parts, oil, pepper, tomatoes, onions — everything I needed to cook Christmas food. That was how we ate that year.

That moment stayed with me. Not because the money was large, but because it arrived when we had nothing left.

The hardship did not end there.

Eventually, I traveled to England after a medical complication and loss. Before the visa came, I dreamed of holding a British pound on a beach. When I woke, I knew I was going.

My suitcase was stolen the night before my flight. I borrowed shoes to travel. I arrived with almost nothing.

In England, I had no legal status, no stable job, and little support. At one point, I was forced out of a relative's home and slept at bus stops. A stranger noticed me waiting too long for a bus one night and insisted on taking me home. That woman became my shelter when I had nowhere else to go.

Not long after, cancer entered my life for the first time.

I underwent surgery and lost my breast. In the hospital, alone at night, the Lord spoke to me. He told me to stop crying. He said my healing would be swift. He said this would not end in shame.

I did not feel strong. I felt broken. But I held on to what He said because it was all I had.

That was how my life continued — between strain and provision, fear and presence, loss and survival.

After the first cancer, I thought I had reached the edge of what a person could endure. I did not know there was more waiting. Life did not pause for my recovery. I still had children to feed, rent to pay, and no legal standing in the country where I lived. Healing did not mean rest. It meant survival with responsibility.

I worked while taking treatment. I did not tell my employers everything. I could not afford to. I took trains for hours to attend hospital appointments and returned to work the same day. My body was weak, but I did not collapse. God gave me strength I did not recognize as strength at the time. I only knew I was still standing.

Church people helped me. Some brought food. Some paid part of my rent. Some gave quietly without asking questions. I did not know many of them well. They knew me enough.

While I was in the hospital, people came—some I had never met before. They brought envelopes, flowers, small gifts. I did not expect it. When I counted everything later, it amounted to thousands of pounds. I had never held that kind of money in my life.

I called my husband in Nigeria. I told him I did not know if I would survive. I told him to use the money to buy land and build a house for the children. I did not want them to be homeless if I died. I prayed over the money before sending it. I did not know how a house could come from what I had. I sent it anyway.

I stayed in England and continued working. I sent money home whenever I could. Slowly, the house began to rise. I cannot explain how it happened. There was no sudden wealth. There was no steady salary. There was only provision, one step at a time.

When I finally returned to Nigeria and saw the house, I could not speak. I walked from room to room in disbelief. I rolled on the floor and cried. I asked God if it was truly mine. It was more than shelter. It was dignity restored.

I remembered the words He spoke years earlier—that He would set a table before me. I understood then that survival is not only about staying alive. It is about being covered.

Life continued again.

Years later, cancer returned.

This time was different. It was during COVID. Hospitals were overwhelmed. People were afraid. When I noticed the change in my breast, it did not look like before. It was swollen, dark, painful. I went to the pharmacy crying, asking strangers what it could be. They did not know.

The doctor confirmed it was cancer. My second breast was removed. When they suggested chemotherapy again, I refused. I was tired. I told them I wanted to die. I did not want to go through it again.

That night, I had a dream.

I saw something being drawn in the sky, like a figure taking shape. It looked like a lion with a mane. He winked at me and said, "I am involved in this. You will not die." He winked again and said He was the Lion of the tribe of Judah.

I woke up angry.

I asked God why He would not let me go. I told Him I had done enough. I told Him my children were grown. I asked what I was still here for. I did not hear an answer I liked, but I knew I would live.

So, I continued treatment.

During that time, my memory failed me often. One day, I left a pot of water boiling on the gas stove and traveled hours away for a hospital appointment. In the middle of the journey, a voice spoke to me and said I had left the pot on the fire. I denied it at first. Then fear took hold of me. I prayed the whole way back.

When I returned home, the pot was still on the fire. The gas had not exploded. The woman I cared for, who had dementia, was still sleeping. Nothing had burned. I cried on the kitchen floor. I did not understand how it was possible.

After surgery, I traveled alone with tubes and bottles draining blood from my body. I asked God to help me move through stations, onto trains, into buses. Each time I needed help, someone appeared. I did not ask. They offered.

One night, I woke and saw an angel standing by my bed. He did not speak. He only stood there. I knew his name without being told.

I learned then that God's presence does not always explain itself. Sometimes it only stays.

That is how my life has unfolded. Not in peace, not in ease, but in presence. I did not choose this journey. I only responded to it.

And I am still here.

When I look back over my life, people often want to know *why* these things happened. They ask what I did right, what prayers I prayed, what I understood that others did not. I never know how to answer that question properly. I did not understand most of what was happening while it was happening. I was not brave. I was not prepared. I was only present.

What stayed with me was not certainty. It was presence.

God did not remove pain from my life. He did not keep death from touching my family. He did not stop betrayal, poverty, illness, or fear. What He did was stay. He stayed when I was a child who did not know Scripture. He stayed when I wanted to die. He stayed when I slept at bus stops. He stayed when my body was cut open and sewn back together. He stayed when my mind failed me and I forgot things that should have been simple.

Many times, I did not feel strong. I felt carried.

I did not always recognize help when it came. Sometimes it looked like a stranger. Sometimes it looked like a word spoken once and never repeated. Sometimes it looked like money I did not earn, a house I did not know how to build, a train I did not know how to navigate alone. I learned that faith is not loud. It does not announce itself. It moves quietly, doing what needs to be done.

I also learned that knowing God does not make you exceptional. It makes you accountable. When He spoke to me, I could not pretend I had not heard. When He intervened, I could not claim credit. When He stayed silent, I still had to live.

There were seasons when I was angry with Him. I told Him I was tired. I told Him I wanted rest. I told Him I had done enough. He did not argue with me. He simply did not leave.

That is what shaped my life more than visions or dreams. Not the moments when heaven opened, but the days when nothing changed and I had to wake up again.

This journey has never been about proving anything. It has been about surviving honestly. About continuing when stopping would have been easier. About trusting a presence I could not control.

I am not telling this story because I am finished. I am telling it because I am still here.

And this is how it began.

2

By the time I decided to leave Nigeria, I was not chasing opportunity. I was running from grief, fear, and the sense that staying might cost me my life. I had buried a child. I had endured medical neglect. I had lived through years of financial strain, emotional exhaustion, and uncertainty. I was not dreaming of a new country. I was trying to survive what I had already been through.

The journey to England did not begin with excitement. It began with loss, desperation, and a decision I made because standing still felt more dangerous than moving.

When the baby died, something shifted inside me.

At the time, life was already very difficult. We could not pay house rent. We could not pay school fees. The children had been locked indoors more than once because we could not afford to let neighbors see how bad things had become. Survival was daily. There was no margin. No backup. No safety.

Then I became pregnant again, and during the pregnancy, I was diagnosed with placenta previa type four.

I went to the hospital. The doctor who was supposed to handle my case was not present when the surgery was carried out. I went in for an operation, and the baby was delivered. She cried when she came out. That gave me hope. But they said she needed more oxygen. They told my husband to go to the blood bank to get blood.

While he was gone, the baby died.

Afterward, there was anger. There was shock. There was grief that felt too heavy to carry. We talked about suing the doctor. He was a powerful man in Nigeria, well known, well connected. When he returned from abroad and learned what had happened, he called us to come and see him.

We met him.

He asked what we wanted him to do. I told him I wanted to go to the United States. He said no. He explained that medical care there would be expensive and that insurance would cost more than we could manage. Instead, he advised that I go to England. He wrote to the British embassy immediately while we were there.

He also wrote to Chelsea Hospital in London. At that point, I had already asked doctors to tie my womb. I did not want to have more children. I was afraid of dying young and leaving the children I already had. I did not want to risk another pregnancy.

He explained my case to the hospital — the loss of the baby, the surgery, the complications. Chelsea Hospital responded quickly. The embassy processed our visas. Before we fully understood what was happening, both my husband and I had visas to travel.

But we could not both go.

We had no money. We had children to care for. We had no place to stay in England. My husband said one of us should go while the other stayed behind to look after the children. He suggested that I go, since I had a stepsister in England and might be able to stay with her briefly.

We did not understand how life worked in England. We had never been there. We did not know how we would survive once I arrived. But the door had opened, and we felt we had to step through it.

Around that time, I began to dream.

In one dream, I saw myself sitting at the tip of an arrow. The arrow was shot across the sky, traveling from Africa to England. I did not know at the time that I was going to England, but in the dream, the arrow carried me there. I landed near a beach.

The water moved toward my feet, washing in and out. As it receded, I saw a British pound coin on the sand. I picked it up and thought, even in the dream, Am I going to England?

In another dream, I saw horses descending from the sky. Traffic stopped. Streets emptied. Everything paused to make way for them. I hid behind a building as they came down. When they reached the ground, they dropped a box in front of me. I opened it, but it was empty. To this day, I do not fully understand what that dream meant.

When the embassy confirmed the visas, my husband said I should go. He said one person must stay behind. The twins were still young. He believed it was better for the children if he remained with them.

We had no money for the plane ticket.

We did not want to tell many people. We were afraid of attracting attention or losing the opportunity. So, we quietly looked for help. A woman who owned a small kiosk near our house lent us some money. A teacher friend gave me money from her savings contribution. Another friend helped cover the rest. Bit by bit, we gathered enough to buy a ticket.

I lived in Benin City, Edo State, so I had to travel to Lagos before flying out.

When we arrived in Lagos and took a taxi to where I was supposed to spend the night, the taxi drove off with all my belongings—my clothes, my shoes, everything. All I had left was my handbag. If my passport had been in the suitcase, I would have lost it too.

I stood there with nothing to wear to London except a pair of slippers.

We begged a security guard for help. He gave me a pair of his trainers. They were too big, but I stuffed them with tissue so they would stay on my feet.

That was how I entered an international airport for the first time in my life.

With borrowed shoes. With almost no belongings. With fear, hope, grief, and faith mixed together.

And that was how I boarded the plane to England.

When I arrived in England, I did not feel settled. I felt alert, cautious, and unsure of what would happen next. I had come with very little, and I knew I could not afford to fail. My children were still in Nigeria. Every decision I made felt tied to their survival.

Before I left Nigeria, I had a dream. In it, I saw myself working for a young couple who had just had a baby. They were medical doctors. That image stayed with me. When I eventually settled in Manchester, I ended up staying with a couple there for one year and two months. In a quiet way, the dream unfolded into real life.

Back home, I had been a teacher. In England, my qualifications did not carry weight. I needed certifications, training, and papers I did not have. Care work was the most accessible option, even for people without full documentation. So I took whatever work I could find.

I worked as a cleaner. I worked in catering. I worked anywhere someone was willing to pay me. I learned quickly because I had no choice. I could not afford pride. I could not afford hesitation.

At one point, I worked as a catering assistant with Manchester United. It was busy, loud, full of movement. One day, David Beckham was present at the stadium. That same day, immigration officers arrived.

I did not know ahead of time. No one warned me. When I realized what was happening, fear took over. I went into the toilet and stayed there for the entire match. Officers arrested many of the workers that day. When I finally came out, my bag was gone. I had no money. I had no way home.

I told the bus driver I had misplaced my wallet. He let me board without paying.

After that incident, I left Manchester. They kept calling me to return to work, but I did not trust it. I believed it could be a trap. I never went back.

Living without legal status meant living with constant awareness. Every knock at the door mattered. Every uniform carried meaning. I learned how to stay unnoticed. I learned how to keep moving without drawing attention.

I worked and sent money home whenever I could. My focus stayed on my children. I wanted them to eat. I wanted them to stay in school. I wanted them to have stability even when I did not.

Then my health began to change.

I was busy working multiple jobs, often exhausted, often running from one place to another. One day, I heard a voice telling me to give thanks to God. I responded with frustration. I felt overwhelmed. I felt stretched thin. Gratitude felt distant.

Not long after, I felt pain under my armpit. Then I noticed a brown substance coming out of my breast. I did not understand what it meant. I did not think of cancer. I thought it might be stress or infection.

Around that time, I had a dream about my aunt. In the dream, she looked frightening. Her mouth was filled with blood. Her appearance unsettled me. I asked her why she wanted to kill me. She did not answer. She walked away.

I did not know how to interpret it. I only knew it stayed with me.

Later, my passport expired, and I returned briefly to Nigeria. While there, I had another dream. In it, cold oil was poured all over me from my head. It even went through me; the pillow I rested my head, even the whole bed—the oil flowed all over. When I told my husband, he said it meant God was setting me apart.

When I returned to England, the physical symptoms grew stronger.

I went to the hospital, even though I had no legal documents. No one questioned me. They sent me for a biopsy. The waiting period felt endless. Four days felt longer than years. My mind ran ahead of me. I thought about my children. I thought about dying far from home.

When the results came back, they told me the cancer was aggressive.

I underwent surgery. My breast was removed. I did not feel prepared. I felt exposed and afraid, but I went through with it because there was no alternative.

After the surgery, while I lay in the hospital, I heard footsteps. A hand touched my shoulder. A voice spoke to me and asked why I was crying. It said, "I am the God of all flesh." The voice told me that what had happened would not end in shame. It told me that something greater would come from it.

My healing was faster than expected. I did not experience the pain many people warned me about. During chemotherapy, I saw a form beside me, holding a basin and squeezing cool water over my head, as if helping me endure the heat and weakness.

When treatment ended, my husband could not come to England. People around me helped. Some gave money. Some gave practical support. I gathered what I received and lifted it up to God in gratitude before sending it home. My husband used the money to buy land and begin building a house for the family.

Even as I recovered, immigration pressure returned. I knew I was still vulnerable. Fear remained part of daily life.

I had a dream where I saw stones arranged across a canal. I crossed them safely, one by one. Later, I had another dream where two large trailers blocked my path. A man dressed in white stepped in and moved them aside so I could pass.

When immigration summoned me to Soho, I remembered those dreams. I felt afraid, but I also felt guided.

My uncle in Hull took me in during that period. At court, they asked for my lawyer. I said my lawyer was present, even though I had none physically beside me. The Home Office did not appear that day. The judge released me and granted leave to remain.

Years later, I became a British citizen. My papers were granted on health and compassionate grounds.

That outcome felt distant from the fear I once lived under. But I never forgot the path that led there.

Even after I received leave to remain, I did not feel settled in a simple way. My status changed, but the weight I carried did not disappear overnight. My children were still far away for a long time. Motherhood became something I lived at a distance, through phone calls, remittances, prayers, and constant concern.

I worked as much as I could. I took jobs others avoided. Care work became a large part of my life. I looked after elderly people, people with dementia, people who could not feed themselves or remember their own names. Sometimes I felt invisible doing that work. Other times, I felt entrusted with something sacred. I stayed because it paid. I stayed because it allowed me to send money home. I stayed because responsibility left me no room to drift.

There were days I felt exhausted beyond words. My body had already been through surgery, chemotherapy, long shifts, sleepless nights, and travel. I did not feel strong. I felt sustained.

God's presence remained steady in the background of my days. Not loud. Not dramatic. Sometimes He spoke through dreams. Sometimes through quiet conviction. Sometimes through interruption—a thought, a warning, a nudge I could not explain.

When immigration pressure resurfaced in different forms over the years, I learned to live with uncertainty without letting it control every decision. The fear did not vanish, but it stopped being the loudest voice in my mind.

The dreams stayed with me.

The stones across the canal. The trailers blocking my path. The man dressed in white making a way forward. I did not always interpret these moments clearly. I only knew that when I felt blocked, something always opened. When I felt cornered, something always shifted.

I thought often about how close I had come to losing everything—my child, my life, my stability, my hope. I remembered the day I boarded a plane with borrowed shoes and no suitcase. I remembered hiding from immigration officers in a stadium toilet. I remembered hearing the word "cancer" when I had no country to call home.

None of it felt theoretical. It was lived.

At times, people asked how I survived it all. I did not have a dramatic answer. I woke up. I worked. I prayed. I endured. Some days I complained. Some days I felt grateful. Some days I felt numb. I kept going.

My faith did not make me fearless. It gave me something to hold when fear showed up. It gave me language when I had no explanation. It gave me restraint when anger would have swallowed me.

There were moments when I questioned why I had been preserved. Why I had been allowed to live when others did not. Why doors kept opening even when I felt undeserving or worn down. I did not always receive answers. I learned to live with the absence of explanation.

Over time, England stopped feeling like a temporary escape and began to feel like a place where my story had unfolded in full. Not as a reward. As a continuation.

I became a British citizen. The paperwork did not erase the past. It marked survival. It marked endurance. It marked a long road that had not broken me.

Still, I did not see myself as someone who had "arrived." I saw myself as someone who had been carried.

And as life continued, I realized that the journey was no longer only about surviving hardship. It was about understanding why I had been kept alive, what I was meant to carry forward, and how to live with a faith shaped by loss, healing, migration, and mercy.

That question stayed with me, even as the next season began.

By the time I became a British citizen, I had already lived several lives in one body.

I had been a daughter, a grieving mother, a wife under strain, an undocumented migrant, a cancer patient, a caregiver, and a woman who learned to survive in unfamiliar systems. The passport and paperwork did not feel like a victory. They felt like a marker along a long road.

My legal status changed, but my awareness did not disappear. I did not forget what it felt like to hide. I did not forget what it meant to depend on kindness from strangers. I did not forget how fragile stability can be.

Through everything, my faith remained shaped more by experience than by theory. God was not an idea to me. He had been present in hospitals, in courtrooms, in taxis, in kitchens, in dreams, in exhaustion, in fear, and in moments where I had nothing left to give.

I learned that faith is not always confident. Sometimes it is tired. Sometimes it is quiet. Sometimes it is simply choosing to stay alive when giving up feels easier.

There were seasons when I wanted rest more than purpose. I told God I was tired. I told Him I had carried enough. I did not feel like a hero. I felt like someone who had been stretched and kept going.

Over time, I began to understand that survival itself can become a calling. Not in a loud or dramatic way, but in the way a person learns to sit with pain, to speak honestly, to carry memory without bitterness, and to live without pretending.

My story did not turn me into someone flawless. It made me more aware of weakness — my own and others'. It made me more patient. It made me more direct. It made me less interested in appearances and more focused on truth.

England became part of my formation. Not because it was easy, but because it tested me, stretched me, and forced me to grow in ways I had not expected.

When I look back now, I do not see a straight path. I see a path shaped by loss, mercy, intervention, endurance, and learning to live with unanswered questions.

And I know this chapter of my life was not only about escape or opportunity. It was about becoming someone who could carry what came next.

I did not come to England to reinvent myself. I came because staying felt unbearable. Over time, this country became the place where my faith was tested, my body was challenged, and my resilience was formed.

This chapter of my life taught me that God's presence does not always come with comfort, but it often comes with endurance. It taught me that survival can carry meaning, even when it feels ordinary. It taught me that I am still here for a reason I did not choose but have learned to accept.

The journey did not end when I received citizenship. It only shifted into a deeper season—one that would ask more questions, bring new challenges, and require a different kind of strength.

That is what the next part of my story begins to explore.

3

By the time my life became more stable on paper, it became less settled in ways I could not explain. I had learned how to survive loss, illness, migration, and uncertainty. I thought the hardest parts were behind me. Instead, a different kind of struggle began to surface—quieter, harder to explain, and more difficult to navigate because it did not announce itself clearly. This season was not about running or arriving. It was about learning discernment, recognizing when peace was absent, and trusting myself to leave even when no one else could see why.

By the time my life became more stable on paper, it became less settled in ways I could not explain. I had learned how to survive loss, illness, migration, and uncertainty. I thought the hardest parts were behind me. Instead, a different kind of struggle began to surface—quieter, harder to explain, and more difficult to navigate because it did not announce itself clearly. This season was not about running or arriving. It was about learning discernment, recognizing when peace was absent, and trusting myself to leave even when no one else could see why.

It began during my placement at a house called Devices. I had gone there as a live-in carer for an elderly man. I was given a room in the house, and no one told me that his wife had already passed away. I only learned that later.

One night, as I lay in bed, a white woman walked past my room. She looked directly at me and then moved toward the direction of the man's bedroom. I did not understand what I was seeing. When I came out to check, there was no one there. Later I realized that the woman I had seen was the man's deceased wife. No one had informed me she had died. That was my first indication that something in that house was not ordinary.

Behind the house was a large park filled with trees and birds. Very often, two birds would come to my window. They did not behave like ordinary birds. I would hear what sounded like human voices as they perched there. I could not make out everything, but it was not natural birdsong. It unsettled me deeply.

As these things continued, I began to pray more intensely. One night while praying, I had a vision of what was beneath the house. I saw a basement where a coven was gathered. In the centre was a large cauldron burning with fire. Around it were leather cushions placed on the floor instead of chairs. I did not know what was inside the pot, but it was burning strongly. I understood in my spirit that there was spiritual activity connected to that house.

It was winter at the time. During one of those nights of prayer, a rainbow appeared at my window. It did not remain outside. It entered the room and covered me completely, even over the duvet as I lay on the bed. I could see its colors around me. It was not faint. It was present and tangible.

The two birds that had been coming to my window did not return after that night. The following morning, the man's son—who had an engineering workshop at the back of the house—found them dead in the compound. They were not in the park. They were inside the property.

He called me and asked if I had seen what had happened. I told him I had not left my room. Later, I was informed that some people in the community had complained that I prayed too much. They believed my prayers were affecting the atmosphere of the house and even the surrounding area. Since I had arrived, they said, unusual things had been happening.

The agency that placed me there was contacted. I was asked to leave. That was how my time at Devices ended.

But the rainbow did not end there.

For nearly a month afterward, I continued seeing rainbows wherever I went. Sometimes they appeared in the sky without rain. On one occasion, as I approached a pharmacy, the colors stretched across the entrance and seemed to cover the doorway before I stepped inside.

During that same period, I noticed that my feet began turning very white. I became afraid. Having battled cancer before, my mind immediately went to illness. I wondered if it was leprosy or if the cancer had returned. I went to see a doctor. After examination, they told me there was nothing medically wrong. I had no pain. There was no infection. There was no diagnosis.

At that time, I did not fully understand what the rainbow signified. Later, I came to believe it was a covenant sign from God—a reassurance of His presence with me. But while I was living through it, I was confused, frightened, and trying to make sense of events that felt far beyond the ordinary.

I then had to move to Bath.

Bath was beautiful. Historic. Calm. When I arrived, I was told I would be caring for a very old woman—at that time, the oldest woman in London. Documentaries had been made about her, though I did not know that then. I did not know anything about her background. I only knew I had been sent there to work.

When she saw me, she was immediately uncomfortable.

She asked why they would send me to take care of her. I did not understand her reaction. I was polite. I was willing. I was grateful to have work. But from the first night, the atmosphere in that house was heavy.

That first night, I did not sleep. It felt like battle. I stayed awake, praying quietly, holding myself together until morning came.

She later instructed me to check on her whenever she went to sleep. One night, I did so at the wrong time. I did not know it then, but she was preparing to do something she did not want interrupted. When she saw me, she reacted violently. She accused me of catching her at the wrong moment. Her anger was sharp and sudden.

The next morning, she called the agency and demanded that I be removed from the house.

Again, I was told to leave.

By then, this pattern had begun to repeat itself. I was placed. I sensed something was wrong. I endured as long as I could. Then I was asked to go. Each time, I left without argument. I did not try to prove anything. I did not accuse anyone. I only knew when I could no longer stay.

I did not yet understand what this season was teaching me. I only knew that I was being kept, even as I was being moved.

By that time, I had learned not to argue when a door closed. I had learned that not every ending needed a defense. Some situations explained themselves only through how they made me feel, and I had come to trust that awareness.

After Bath, the agency continued to place me in different homes. Each assignment came with its own tension. Some were subtle, some immediate. In one house, the son of the woman I cared for traveled abroad, leaving me alone with her. She did not like me from the beginning, though she tolerated my presence. I completed the four weeks assigned to me and left quietly. That placement ended without drama, but not without strain.

Another placement ended more abruptly.

I was sent to care for an elderly couple. The husband was eighty-seven years old and lived with Parkinson's disease. His body shook constantly, and his speech was difficult to understand. I was patient with him. I spoke gently. Over time, he became comfortable with me. He treated me like a daughter.

That closeness disturbed his wife.

From the first day, she resisted my presence. She questioned why I had been brought into their home. She said I carried a contrary spirit. At the time, I did not fully understand what she meant. I focused on my work. I kept my distance. I tried to make myself small.

One night, I had a dream.

In the dream, the woman came toward me with aggression. I was given a long whip, placed directly into my hand. A voice told me to warn her not to come any closer. I spoke the warning aloud in the dream. She continued toward me. When she came close, I struck her once with the whip. She turned and fled.

I woke up early the next morning. When I opened my door, she stood there smiling, greeting me as if nothing had happened. I answered politely and went about my work. I sang quietly as I worked, without intention, without performance.

Her mood shifted.

When her son arrived later that day, she cried and demanded that I leave the house. The son refused. He said I should complete the four weeks agreed upon. She endured my presence, but the atmosphere remained tense until I left.

After that placement ended, something changed.

From 2021 onward, I stopped receiving work.

I applied for jobs I had done for years. I was told I was no longer qualified. Agencies said clients had chosen someone else. Some said the job had been canceled altogether. The pattern repeated itself over months, then years.

I did not accuse anyone openly. I did not name causes I could not prove. I only knew that something had shifted after that season. Work dried up. Stability slipped away again.

I examined myself. I prayed. I waited.

I did not feel abandoned, but I felt paused.

This season forced me to confront a different kind of endurance. Not the endurance of running from crisis to crisis, but the endurance of standing still when nothing moved. I had to learn how to trust God without visible momentum, without income, without clarity.

I also had to learn restraint. Not every battle is fought by confrontation. Some are navigated through silence and distance.

Looking back, I can see that this period sharpened my discernment. It taught me to recognize when something was not meant for me, even if it looked like provision. It taught me to leave without anger and to accept loss without needing to justify myself.

I did not yet know that there was another experience waiting—one that would bring this season to a clearer close.

By the time I was sent to Chelsea, I had learned not to expect clarity at the beginning of an assignment. I arrived with the same quiet discipline I always carried—observe first, speak little, do the work in front of me. The placement appeared ordinary on paper. The home was well-kept. The surroundings were comfortable. Nothing immediately suggested trouble.

Still, something felt off.

The woman I was sent to care for presented herself with confidence. She spoke clearly. She was articulate and commanding. From the start, she asked many questions about me—where I came from, what I believed, how I prayed. I answered carefully. I did not volunteer information. I did not challenge her. I stayed within my role.

The unease did not come from anything she said directly. It came from what lingered underneath our interactions. Conversations carried weight. Silences felt deliberate. I found myself watching my words more closely than usual, measuring not only what I said but how it might be received.

At night, my sleep was restless.

I began to sense the same internal warning I had felt in previous places. It did not come as fear. It came as pressure. A tightening. A sense that staying too long would cost something I could not afford to lose.

I prayed quietly, asking for clarity. Not a sign. Not confirmation through drama. Just enough understanding to know whether I should stay or leave.

What came instead was restraint.

I was not told to confront. I was not told to accuse. I was not told to explain myself. I was simply aware that I should not remain.

I completed what I could of my duties. I remained respectful. I did not escalate anything. When the opportunity came to leave, I took it without hesitation.

After that placement, work did not resume.

Time passed. Weeks turned into months. The calls stopped. I followed up with agencies and received vague responses. Sometimes I received none at all. The silence confirmed what I had already sensed—that this chapter of my work life had ended.

For the first time in years, I was not being moved from place to place. I was standing still.

This stillness forced reflection. I replayed events in my mind, not obsessively, but honestly. I asked myself if I had imagined things. If I had overreacted. If fear had shaped my decisions.

Each time I returned to the same conclusion: I had not acted in panic. I had acted in preservation.

I began to understand that discernment does not always come with reassurance. Sometimes it comes with loss. Sometimes it comes with misunderstanding. Sometimes it costs livelihood and comfort.

But it also protects life.

Looking back, I see that this season was not about confrontation or victory. It was about learning the difference between endurance and exposure. About knowing when faith means staying and when it means stepping away.

By the end of this chapter, I did not feel triumphant. I felt quieter. More aware. Less willing to force myself into places where peace did not exist.

I did not yet know what the next season would require of me. I only knew that this one had ended.

It began during my placement at a house called Devices. I had gone there as a live-in carer for an elderly man. I was given a room in the house, and no one told me that his wife had already passed away. I only learned that later.

One night, as I lay in bed, a white woman walked past my room. She looked directly at me and then moved toward the direction of the man's bedroom. I did not understand what I was seeing. When I came out to check, there was no one there. Later I realized that the woman I had seen was the man's deceased wife. No one had informed me she had died. That was my first indication that something in that house was not ordinary.

Behind the house was a large park filled with trees and birds. Very often, two birds would come to my window. They did not behave like ordinary birds. I would hear what sounded like human voices as they perched there. I could not make out everything, but it was not natural birdsong. It unsettled me deeply.

As these things continued, I began to pray more intensely. One night while praying, I had a vision of what was beneath the house. I saw a basement where a coven was gathered. In the centre was a large cauldron burning with fire. Around it were leather cushions placed on the floor instead of chairs. I did not know what was inside the pot, but it was burning strongly. I understood in my spirit that there was spiritual activity connected to that house.

It was winter at the time. During one of those nights of prayer, a rainbow appeared at my window. It did not remain outside. It entered the room and covered me completely, even over the duvet as I lay on the bed. I could see its colors around me. It was not faint. It was present and tangible.

The two birds that had been coming to my window did not return after that night. The following morning, the man's son—who had an engineering workshop at the back of the house—found them dead in the compound. They were not in the park. They were inside the property.

He called me and asked if I had seen what had happened. I told him I had not left my room. Later, I was informed that some people in the community had complained that I prayed too much. They believed my prayers were affecting the atmosphere of the house and even the surrounding area. Since I had arrived, they said, unusual things had been happening.

The agency that placed me there was contacted. I was asked to leave. That was how my time at Devices ended.

But the rainbow did not end there.

For nearly a month afterward, I continued seeing rainbows wherever I went. Sometimes they appeared in the sky without rain. On one occasion, as I approached a pharmacy, the colors stretched across the entrance and seemed to cover the doorway before I stepped inside.

During that same period, I noticed that my feet began turning very white. I became afraid. Having battled cancer before, my mind immediately went to illness. I wondered if it was leprosy or if the cancer had returned. I went to see a doctor. After examination, they told me there was nothing medically wrong. I had no pain. There was no infection. There was no diagnosis.

At that time, I did not fully understand what the rainbow signified. Later, I came to believe it was a covenant sign from God—a reassurance of His presence with me. But while I was living through it, I was confused, frightened, and trying to make sense of events that felt far beyond the ordinary.

I then had to move to Bath.

Bath was beautiful. Historic. Calm. When I arrived, I was told I would be caring for a very old woman—at that time, the oldest woman in London. Documentaries had been made about her, though I did not know that then. I did not know anything about her background. I only knew I had been sent there to work.

When she saw me, she was immediately uncomfortable.

She asked why they would send me to take care of her. I did not understand her reaction. I was polite. I was willing. I was grateful to have work. But from the first night, the atmosphere in that house was heavy.

That first night, I did not sleep. It felt like battle. I stayed awake, praying quietly, holding myself together until morning came.

She later instructed me to check on her whenever she went to sleep. One night, I did so at the wrong time. I did not know it then, but she was preparing to do something she did not want interrupted. When she saw me, she reacted violently. She accused me of catching her at the wrong moment. Her anger was sharp and sudden.

The next morning, she called the agency and demanded that I be removed from the house.

Again, I was told to leave.

By then, this pattern had begun to repeat itself. I was placed. I sensed something was wrong. I endured as long as I could. Then I was asked to go. Each time, I left without argument. I did not try to prove anything. I did not accuse anyone. I only knew when I could no longer stay.

I did not yet understand what this season was teaching me. I only knew that I was being kept, even as I was being moved.

By that time, I had learned not to argue when a door closed. I had learned that not every ending needed a defense. Some situations explained themselves only through how they made me feel, and I had come to trust that awareness.

After Bath, the agency continued to place me in different homes. Each assignment came with its own tension. Some were subtle, some immediate. In one house, the son of the woman I cared for traveled abroad, leaving me alone with her.

She did not like me from the beginning, though she tolerated my presence. I completed the four weeks assigned to me and left quietly. That placement ended without drama, but not without strain.

Another placement ended more abruptly.

I was sent to care for an elderly couple. The husband was eighty-seven years old and lived with Parkinson's disease. His body shook constantly, and his speech was difficult to understand. I was patient with him. I spoke gently. Over time, he became comfortable with me. He treated me like a daughter.

That closeness disturbed his wife.

From the first day, she resisted my presence. She questioned why I had been brought into their home. She said I carried a contrary spirit. At the time, I did not fully understand what she meant. I focused on my work. I kept my distance. I tried to make myself small.

One night, I had a dream.

In the dream, the woman came toward me with aggression. I was given a long whip, placed directly into my hand. A voice told me to warn her not to come any closer. I spoke the warning aloud in the dream. She continued toward me. When she came close, I struck her once with the whip. She turned and fled.

I woke up early the next morning. When I opened my door, she stood there smiling, greeting me as if nothing had happened. I answered politely and went about my work. I sang quietly as I worked, without intention, without performance.

Her mood shifted.

When her son arrived later that day, she cried and demanded that I leave the house. The son refused. He said I should complete the four weeks agreed upon. She endured my presence, but the atmosphere remained tense until I left.

After that placement ended, something changed.

From 2021 onward, I stopped receiving work.

I applied for jobs I had done for years. I was told I was no longer qualified. Agencies said clients had chosen someone else. Some said the job had been canceled altogether. The pattern repeated itself over months, then years.

I did not accuse anyone openly. I did not name causes I could not prove. I only knew that something had shifted after that season. Work dried up. Stability slipped away again.

I examined myself. I prayed. I waited.

I did not feel abandoned, but I felt paused.

This season forced me to confront a different kind of endurance. Not the endurance of running from crisis to crisis, but the endurance of standing still when nothing moved. I had to learn how to trust God without visible momentum, without income, without clarity.

I also had to learn restraint. Not every battle is fought by confrontation. Some are navigated through silence and distance.

Looking back, I can see that this period sharpened my discernment. It taught me to recognize when something was not meant for me, even if it looked like provision. It taught me to leave without anger and to accept loss without needing to justify myself.

I did not yet know that there was another experience waiting—one that would bring this season to a clearer close.

By the time I was sent to Chelsea, I had learned not to expect clarity at the beginning of an assignment. I arrived with the same quiet discipline I always carried—observe first, speak little, do the work in front of me. The placement appeared ordinary on paper. The home was well-kept. The surroundings were comfortable. Nothing immediately suggested trouble.

Still, something felt off.

The woman I was sent to care for presented herself with confidence. She spoke clearly. She was articulate and commanding. From the start, she asked many questions about me—where I came from, what I believed, how I prayed. I answered carefully. I did not volunteer information. I did not challenge her. I stayed within my role.

The unease did not come from anything she said directly. It came from what lingered underneath our interactions. Conversations carried weight. Silences felt deliberate. I found myself watching my words more closely than usual, measuring not only what I said but how it might be received.

At night, my sleep was restless.

I began to sense the same internal warning I had felt in previous places. It did not come as fear. It came as pressure. A tightening. A sense that staying too long would cost something I could not afford to lose.

I prayed quietly, asking for clarity. Not a sign. Not confirmation through drama. Just enough understanding to know whether I should stay or leave.

What came instead was restraint.

I was not told to confront. I was not told to accuse. I was not told to explain myself. I was simply aware that I should not remain.

I completed what I could of my duties. I remained respectful. I did not escalate anything. When the opportunity came to leave, I took it without hesitation.

After that placement, work did not resume.

Time passed. Weeks turned into months. The calls stopped. I followed up with agencies and received vague responses. Sometimes I received none at all. The silence confirmed what I had already sensed—that this chapter of my work life had ended.

For the first time in years, I was not being moved from place to place. I was standing still.

This stillness forced reflection. I replayed events in my mind, not obsessively, but honestly. I asked myself if I had imagined things. If I had overreacted. If fear had shaped my decisions.

Each time I returned to the same conclusion: I had not acted in panic. I had acted in preservation.

I began to understand that discernment does not always come with reassurance. Sometimes it comes with loss. Sometimes it comes with misunderstanding. Sometimes it costs livelihood and comfort.

But it also protects life.

Looking back, I see that this season was not about confrontation or victory. It was about learning the difference between endurance and exposure. About knowing when faith means staying and when it means stepping away.

By the end of this chapter, I did not feel triumphant. I felt quieter. More aware. Less willing to force myself into places where peace did not exist.

I did not yet know what the next season would require of me. I only knew that this one had ended.

4

By this point in my life, I had already learned that not every struggle announces itself as danger. Some arrive quietly, wrapped in routine, disguised as responsibility. This chapter begins in a season where I was no longer running, no longer undocumented, no longer recovering from illness. On the surface, things looked stable. I was working. I was housed. I was functioning.

What changed was not my circumstances as much as the cost of remaining where I was not meant to stay. This was the season when obedience became expensive, when restraint mattered more than explanation, and when walking away carried consequences I could not soften or avoid.

Care work had taught me how to live inside other people's lives without taking up too much space. You enter someone's home, follow their routines, learn their habits, and make yourself useful without being seen as intrusive. Over the years, I became good at that. I knew how to be present without overstepping.

But some placements did not stay contained within daylight hours.

There were homes where the atmosphere shifted as soon as night came. Nothing obvious changed. The rooms were the same. The furniture did not move. But my body registered something different. Sleep became shallow. I woke often. Sometimes I did not sleep at all.

I learned to sit quietly in the dark and pray without words, not because I was afraid in the way people imagine fear, but because something felt active, unsettled, unresolved.

One placement brought this into sharper focus.

The house itself was old and well kept. The client was frail, dependent, and mostly quiet during the day. There was nothing in her behavior that explained what happened at night. When evening came and the house settled, I felt pressure. Not noise. Not movement. Pressure.

I stayed awake, holding myself steady, asking God for protection without asking questions I did not need answered. By morning, my body felt as though I had been awake all night, even when I could not remember moving.

This happened more than once.

I did not report it. I did not dramatize it. I continued to work. But I paid attention.

Over time, I realized that these experiences followed a pattern. They did not occur everywhere. They appeared in certain homes, with certain individuals, and then disappeared when I left. That mattered to me. It told me that I was not unraveling. Something external was interacting with me.

I was careful not to assign blame or meaning too quickly. I did not label people. I did not accuse. I focused on discernment rather than interpretation.

Then came the placement that forced clarity.

I was sent to care for a couple. The husband's condition required constant attention. Parkinson's had taken much from him, but not his gentleness. He relied on me for daily care, and over time he relaxed into that dependence. I treated him with the respect I would want shown to my own father.

His wife watched closely.

Her resistance was immediate and unhidden. She questioned my presence, my demeanor, my beliefs. She spoke about energy and influence in a way that felt deliberate. I remained calm. I kept my responses neutral. I did my work and avoided unnecessary conversation.

At night, the pressure returned.

One night, the dream came.

It was not symbolic in the way people often describe dreams. It was direct. The woman approached me aggressively. I was given a whip—not in anger, not for attack, but as a boundary. I was told to warn her. I did. She did not stop. When she crossed the line, I struck her once, and she fled.

I woke early, fully alert.

When I opened my door later that morning, she stood there smiling, greeting me as though nothing had happened. Her demeanor was calm, pleasant, even warm. I returned the greeting and went about my work.

As I worked, I sang quietly. Not for her. Not as a statement. It simply came out of me.

Her reaction was immediate.

By the time her son arrived, she was crying, accusing me of disturbing her peace, demanding that I be removed. The son intervened, insisting I complete the agreed period. I stayed until the placement ended, but the atmosphere never eased.

After that, something closed.

Work stopped coming. Agencies that had relied on me for years stopped calling. Applications led nowhere. Explanations were vague or absent. It was as though a door had shut without ceremony.

This was no longer about discomfort. It was about consequence.

I understood then that obedience does not always end in reassurance. Sometimes it ends in loss. Sometimes it costs livelihood. Sometimes it isolates you.

But I also understood that staying would have cost more.

After work stopped, the quiet around me became louder than any confrontation I had avoided. There were no formal explanations, no accusations made to my face, no incident reports I could point to. What existed instead was absence—of calls, of placements, of opportunity. I had lived long enough inside systems to recognize when something had shifted beneath the surface.

This was not confusion. It was consequence.

I replayed events carefully, not to punish myself, but to understand where restraint had been required and where silence had protected me. I knew better than to speak loosely about spiritual matters. I knew the cost of misnaming experiences or assigning motives without certainty. What I carried could not be reduced to complaint.

So I said very little.

People around me noticed the change in my circumstances and asked questions. I gave measured answers. I said work had slowed. I said I was waiting. I did not try to convince anyone that something had been taken from me unfairly. I did not want validation that came at the price of exaggeration.

This season demanded discipline.

There were moments when I wanted to explain myself fully, to describe the pressure at night, the dreams, the sense of being watched, the sudden reversals. But I understood that not everyone has language for these things, and not everyone needs to. Some truths are not strengthened by repetition. They are weakened.

I learned that silence can be a boundary just as firm as distance.

In the midst of this stillness, my faith shifted again. Prayer became less about asking for movement and more about asking for clarity. I did not ask to return to work at any cost. I asked to be kept from situations that would undo me.

There were days when fear crept in quietly. Not the sharp fear of danger, but the dull fear of stagnation. I worried about money. I worried about the future. I worried about becoming invisible in a system that once depended on me.

Yet beneath those worries, there was a steadiness I could not deny.

I did not feel abandoned.

I felt guarded.

This distinction mattered. Abandonment drains hope. Guarding preserves it, even when nothing else is visible. I sensed that what had closed was not meant to reopen, and that pressing against it would lead nowhere good.

I began to understand that some seasons of loss are preventative. They stop you from walking further into something that would demand more than you should give.

The Chelsea placement returned to my mind often during this time. Not as a failure, but as a line I had not crossed. I had not accused. I had not confronted. I had not escalated. I had left when restraint demanded it.

That mattered more than being understood.

As weeks passed, I stopped waiting for the phone to ring. I shifted my attention inward, listening more carefully to my own limits. I paid attention to my health, my energy, my thoughts. I learned to sit with uncertainty without forcing meaning onto it.

This season stripped away any illusion that faith guarantees stability. What it offers instead is alignment—the ability to recognize when something is out of order and to step back without spectacle.

I did not know then what would come next. I only knew that whatever remained ahead would require a different posture than endurance alone.

As time passed, the loss of work became more than a practical problem. It settled into my body. I felt it in the way my days stretched without structure, in the way silence filled spaces once occupied by routine. I had always measured time by responsibility—who needed care, what task came next, where I was required. Without that, I had to confront myself without distraction.

Isolation grew quietly.

It was not the dramatic loneliness of abandonment. People still existed around me. Life continued. But the sense of purpose that had anchored me through instability was no longer there. I was no longer needed in the same way. That absence carried its own grief.

I examined myself honestly. I asked whether I had misunderstood what I experienced. Whether caution had turned into withdrawal. Whether obedience had cost more than it preserved. These questions did not accuse me; they tested me. I sat with them instead of answering too quickly.

I noticed how easily people expect resolution. They want stories to end with clarity, with justice neatly served, with doors reopening. This season did not offer that. It offered endurance without explanation.

At times, anger surfaced—not toward people, but toward the situation itself. I had worked faithfully. I had carried responsibility well. I had avoided conflict. Still, the outcome was loss. Accepting that required maturity I did not feel equipped for, but I grew into it slowly.

My faith became less expressive and more internal. I spoke less about spiritual matters and listened more. I did not withdraw from God; I leaned into Him differently. Not asking Him to fix what had broken, but to steady me where I stood.

There were moments when I felt invisible. Moments when I questioned whether my obedience had made me expendable. Those thoughts passed, but they left their mark. They taught me how easily identity can become tied to usefulness.

I learned to detach worth from function.

This season also sharpened my awareness of boundaries. I became more selective about where I placed myself, how much I gave, and what I tolerated. I no longer believed that endurance alone was proof of faith. Sometimes wisdom shows itself through refusal.

What remained with me was not fear, but caution shaped by experience. I trusted myself more. I trusted silence. I trusted the instinct to step back before damage occurred.

Looking back, I see that this was not a collapse. It was a narrowing. A reduction that stripped away excess and forced me to carry only what mattered.